A New Tune A Day

Pop Performance Pieces

for Flute

Chord symbols for all pieces are included
for guitar or keyboard accompaniment.

Boston Music Company
Part of The Music Sales Group
London/New York/Paris/Sydney/Copenhagen/Berlin/Madrid/Hong Kong/Tokyo

Contents

Published by

Boston Music Company

Exclusive Distributors:

Music Sales Limited

14-15 Berners Street, London W1T 3LJ, UK.

Music Sales Corporation

257 Park Avenue South, New York, NY 10010, USA.

Music Sales Pty Limited

20 Resolution Drive, Caringbah, NSW 2229, Australia.

Order No. BM12650
ISBN: 978-1-78038-508-2

Produced by shedwork.com
Photography by Matthew Ward

Printed in the EU

Your Guarantee of Quality

As publishers, we strive to produce every book to the highest commercial standards. The music has been freshly engraved and the book has been carefully designed to minimise awkward page turns and to make playing from it a real pleasure. Throughout, the printing and binding have been planned to ensure a sturdy, attractive publication which should give years of enjoyment. If your copy fails to meet our high standards, please inform us and we will gladly replace it.

www.musicsales.com

Bad Romance

Words & Music by Stefani Germanotta & RedOne

With confidence ♩ = 119

(hi-hat cue)

N.C.

4

Brown Eyed Girl

Words & Music by Van Morrison

Candle In The Wind

Words & Music by Elton John & Bernie Taupin

D.S. al Coda

Dancing Queen

Words & Music by Benny Andersson,
Stig Anderson & Björn Ulvaeus

Moderate rock

Repeat and fade

Hallelujah

Words & Music by Leonard Cohen
© Copyright 1984 Sony/ATV Music Publishing.
All Rights Reserved. International Copyright Secured.

6

Expressively ♩. = 61

mp cantabile

cresc. poco a poco

f

mf espressivo

A tempo

I Believe I Can Fly

Words & Music by R Kelly

© Copyright 1997 Zomba Songs Incorporated, USA
Imagem Music.
All Rights Reserved. International Copyright Secured.

Slow but rhythmic

I Got You (I Feel Good)

Words & Music by James Brown

© Copyright 1966 Fort Knox Music Company, USA.
Lark Music Limited.
All Rights Reserved. International Copyright Secured.

Medium fast tempo

(I've Had) The Time Of My Life

Words & Music by Frankie Previte,
John DeNicola & Donald Markowitz

cresc. poco a poco

10 Imagine

Words & Music by John Lennon
© Copyright 1971 Lenono Music.
All Rights Reserved. International Copyright Secured.

Medium slow (♩ = 76)

Tenderly ♩ = 119

Someone Like You

Words & Music by Adele Adkins & Daniel Wilson

Smoothly, with tenderness ♩ = 68

32

13 *Man In The Mirror*

Steadily, with a bounce ♩ = 100

Stand By Me

Words & Music by Ben E. King, Jerry Leiber & Mike Stoller

Medium fast tempo

With A Little Help From My Friends

Words & Music by
John Lennon & Paul McCartney
© Copyright 1967 Sony/ATV Music Publishing.
All Rights Reserved. International Copyright Secured.

With a relaxed lilt ♩ = 107

mf leggiero

17 *Viva La Vida*

Words & Music by Guy Berryman, Jon Buckland, Will Champion & Chris Martin

Lightly ♩ = 138

123456789

CD backing tracks

1. **TUNING NOTE**

2. **BAD ROMANCE**
(Germanotta/RedOne)
Sony/ATV Music Publishing (UK) Limited

3. **BROWN EYED GIRL**
(Morrison)
Universal Music Publishing Limited

4. **CANDLE IN THE WIND**
(John/Taupin)
Universal/Dick James Music Limited

5. **DANCING QUEEN**
(Andersson/Anderson/Ulvaeus)
Bocu Music Limited

6. **HALLELUJAH**
(Cohen)
Sony/ATV Music Publishing (UK) Limited

7. **I BELIEVE I CAN FLY**
(Kelly)
Imagem Music

8. **I GOT YOU (I FEEL GOOD)**
(Brown)
Lark Music Limited

9. **(I'VE HAD) THE TIME OF MY LIFE**
(Previte/DeNicola/Markowitz)
Worldsong Incorporated/Sony/ATV Music Publishing (UK) Limited/
EMI Music Publishing Limited/Songs Of Pen UK

10. **IMAGINE**
(Lennon)
Lenono Music

11. **LOVE STORY**
(Swift)
Sony/ATV Music Publishing (UK) Limited

12. **SOMEONE LIKE YOU**
(Adkins/Wilson)
Universal Music Publishing Limited/Chrysalis Music Limited

13. **MAN IN THE MIRROR**
(Ballard/Garrett)
Universal/MCA Music Limited/Cherry Lane Music Limited

14. **STAND BY ME**
(King/Leiber/Stoller)
Sony/ATV Music Publishing (UK) Limited

15. **WITH A LITTLE HELP FROM MY FRIENDS**
(Lennon/McCartney)
Sony/ATV Music Publishing (UK) Limited

16. **TAKE A BOW**
(Eriksen/Hermansen/Smith)
Imagem Music/EMI Music Publishing Limited/
Sony/ATV Music Publishing (UK) Limited

17. **VIVA LA VIDA**
(Berryman/Buckland/Champion/Martin)
Universal Music Publishing MGB Limited

How to use the CD

The tuning note on track 1 is an A.

After track 1, the backing tracks are listed in the order in which they appear in the book. Look for the 💿 symbol in the book for the relevant backing track.